SERVANTS OF LOVE

The Spirituality of Teresa of Ávila

By the same author

The Great Teresa
Héloïse
The Desert My Dwelling Place
(A Study of Charles de Foucauld)
I Stay in the Church
Cardinal Suenens: A Portrait

SERVANTS OF LOVE

The Spirituality of Teresa of Ávila

Edited and Introduced by
ELIZABETH HAMILTON

DARTON, LONGMAN AND TODD

1975

First published in Great Britain in 1975 by
Darton, Longman and Todd Ltd
85 Gloucester Road, London SW7 4SU

Printed in Great Britain by The Anchor Press Ltd
and bound by Wm Brendon & Son Ltd
both of Tiptree, Essex

ISBN 0 232 51313 9

CONTENTS

NOTE

The translations from the Spanish are my own with the exception of the verse on p.103, which has been translated by Fr Anselm, O.D.C.

So as not to distort the message contained in the often long pasages from which these excerpts are chosen, I have taken the liberty from time to time of omitting or inserting a word or a phrase.

References are given, and, in the case of letters, the name of the recipient and, where possible, the date.

ELIZABETH HAMILTON

PART ONE

Introduction

TERESA OF ÁVILA

'To understand our saint, you must look at Castile.' The speaker was a priest wearing the brown habit of a Discalced Carmelite who talked to me in the train between Madrid and Ávila on an afternoon in early April. The skin was drawn tight across his forehead and high cheekbones, as though he had lived continually exposed to scorching heat or shrivelling winds.

When we reached Ávila great soft snowflakes drifted upon the dusk. Snow made patches of white upon the cobbles and lay in drifts where the crenellated walls bulged into drum-shaped turrets, each reminiscent of a giant castle on a chess-board. Flakes settled on the black hide of a pair of oxen drawing a wooden cart, their bells tinkling, the cumbersome wheels jolting and creaking. A shepherd passed, wrapped in a brown plaid shawl. I was aware of the smell of wood-smoke and the laughter of children under an arched gateway.

In the morning snow was still lying. It was visible, too, on the summit of mountains across the vast, purple-shadowed Castilian plain. But the mildness of the air and the brightness of the sunlight washing the battlements to the golden pallor of ripening barley told me that winter was past. Storks soared on silk-white wings. Others sat up awkwardly in a nest of sticks piled high on the belfry of the convent of Santa Ana which, with its barred windows and thick walls, suggested a fortress rather than a house for religious. A donkey laden with small fat milk churns in baskets stopped of its own accord from door to door, followed by a second straddled with sacks containing loaves. In the Plaza de Santa Teresa the romanesque church of San Pedro was the colour of dried apricots. Beside it, taller than the building, were two acacia trees, their buds a haze of gold. In front were small heraldic lions carved out of granite.

Doña Teresa de Cepeda y Ahumada was born in Ávila on 28 March 1515.

Her father, Don Alonso Sanchez de Cepeda, recorded the date in a book in which he used to put down the birthdays of his children. There was Jewish blood on her father's side of the family, which may have contributed to her exceptional intelligence as well as to an exaggerated sense of guilt – a trait commonly found among Christians who traced their descent from those who, in Teresa's day, were stamped as deicides. Her mother came of an ancient, aristocratic family of Ávila.

Don Alonso was a man of courage, integrity and a self-discipline which did not deter him from taking pride in his violet and crimson doublets and his shirts embroidered in gold. Moreover, such was his compassion that, unlike the majority of his contemporaries, he could not bring himself to own a slave. When for a while he looked after a slave-girl belonging to a brother of his, he treated her as though she were one of the family.

He was a great reader, as also was his wife Doña Beatrix Davila y Ahumada. But whereas he preferred serious works – religious books and the classics of ancient Rome – she chose romantic tales of chivalry, then much in vogue, telling of knights and their ladies : stories which shocked the moralists but gave pleasure to the young Ignatius Loyola. Furthermore, she encouraged her children to read these romances, hoping, Teresa says, to keep them from worse pastimes. Indeed, Teresa became obsessed with stories of this kind. She read them day and night – as far as possible without her father's knowledge, for Don Alonso disapproved. To Doña Beatrix the romances provided a form of escape. For although Teresa's mother was both intelligent and beautiful, she was saddened in youth by the loss of her father and brothers and, in her married life, by constant illness. She read, her daughter tells us, 'to escape from her great trials'.

Teresa, to the end of her life, loved her native city : the battlements, the gateways, the *palacios* with their barred windows, nail-studded doors, and carved escutcheons. Ávila of the knights. *Ávila de los Caballeros.* Down the centuries it had been the scene of much fighting. Indeed, the *palacios* – each charged with the city's defence – provided for Teresa, when she wrote about the spiritual life, a symbol of what a contemplative convent should be : 'a fortress manned with a chosen company of the king's soldiers'.

There is a saying in Ávila *'una puerta, un palacio'* : 'where there is a gate, there you will find a mansion'. And Teresa's home was close to one of the gates. From childhood she had looked down over a landscape of savage boulders and, then, the treeless plain reaching on and on to mountains sharp as a flint edge against the sky. Winters were bitter, the heat of summer intense. Light was hard, shadows clear-cut. No half-tones, no softness. It was a landscape that helped to mould a people to whom life presented itself in extremes. *Todo o nada.* All or nothing. Heat or cold. Light or darkness. Truth or falsehood. God or the devil. Heaven or hell.

As a small child Teresa and her brother Rodrigo talked about the prospect of an eternity that would be either

13

bliss or pain. They used to chant : *'Para siempre, siempre, siempre'.* 'For ever, for ever, for ever.' Then, one day, determined to be assured of bliss, they set out for the land of the Moors, seeking martyrdom – only to be brought back ignominiously by an uncle on horseback who overtook them on the road to Salamanca. Their mother, who had been distraught with anxiety, rebuked Rodrigo as being the elder – to which he retorted indignantly : *'La niña* made me do it.'

When her mother died, Teresa was thirteen. She says she was twelve, but she had 'no head for dates'. In her grief she turned to the Blessed Virgin. She used to pray before a statue known as *La Virgen de la Caridad,* in the hermitage of *San Segundo,* a little way outside the city. Today the statue is in the cathedral. In the glimmering light of tapers the black eyes stare; the smile is stiff, like the smile of a doll; the brocade skirt stands out in the shape of a bell.

Teresa's adolescence was tempestuous. She spent much time with cousins : the three sons and the daughter of Doña Elvira de Cepeda, the rich, widowed sister of Don Alonso.* He, it is true, had misgivings about his nephews and niece, whose upbringing had been more sophisticated than that of his own children. He could not, however, close his home to his relations. Besides, he was glad that Teresa, his favourite child, should have company of her own age – if only to compensate in some small degree for the sadness caused by her mother's death.

Teresa was delighted with her cousins. She listened enthralled to the tales of their escapades and flirtations.

*See Padre Efrén de la Madre de Dios, *Biografía de Santa Teresa, Obras de Santa Teresa, Biblioteca de Autores Cristianos*, Vol. I, p. 283.

And she, in turn, delighted them with her quick wit and repartee.

During the *processes* which lead to the canonisation of Teresa along with that of Ignatius Loyola in the year 1622, a nun, giving evidence, recalled her as a girl with sparkling black eyes, arched eyebrows, wearing an orange dress trimmed with black galloons. Teresa liked pretty clothes and jewelry. In a letter to her brother Lorenzo, written some thirty years later, she says: 'I kiss my brother's hands a thousand times for the gift he has sent me. If the medallion had come in the days when I wore golden ornaments, I would have coveted it no end – it is absolutely charming.'

When, long after this, she was asked by her confessor to write her *Life* she was forbidden to recount in detail the 'wickedness', the 'deception', the 'iniquities', of which, she says, she was guilty in girlhood. Her confessor's attitude is understandable, but the result is unfortunate. Specific instances of her wrong doings are not given. Worse, the reader is confronted with a baffling entanglement of hints, innuendoes and insinuations which can only have the effect of whetting to no purpose the reader's curiosity.

For most people adolescence is a time of stress, and Teresa's was no exception. Besides having lost her mother, she was faced with having to make a decision. What was she to do with her life? She was afraid, she says, of marriage. And no wonder, if she saw it in terms of her mother Doña Beatrix – a gifted woman, exhausted with child-bearing, withdrawing more and more into a romantic world of make-believe.

But neither did Teresa want to be a nun.

And what else had sixteenth-century Spain to offer? Nothing. Nothing, that is to say, unless she were to become a *beata* and risk turning into an eccentric, such as, for example, Catalina de Cardona, who, after being for a while governess to the son of King Philip II, lived alone in a cave, signed herself, Teresa tells us, *La Peccadora,* fed on leaves and roots, wore a hair-shirt which made her look like a man – and, to crown all, was visited by the devil in the form of a mastiff.

After much heart-searching and bouts of illness which today would be described as psychosomatic, Teresa decided to become a nun. Her choice, she reflected, would mean a life of purgatory. But it would also mean an eternity of joy. She was still the child who had thought martyrdom worthwhile, if, awaiting her, was an eternity of bliss.

And so in the chill November dawn of All Souls, 1536, accompanied by a younger brother who was intending to try his vocation as a friar, she made her way on foot to the Carmelite Convent of the Incarnation about half a mile outside Ávila. Such was her distress that the agony of death could not, she says, have been greater. It was as if her bones were being wrenched asunder. Nor did she feel any love of God to console her for the loss of father and kinsfolk.

*

It is a unique experience to stand on the city's ramparts in the shimmering midday heat of summer, in a silence broken only by the cicadas' monotonous chorus – to look down, beyond red roofs and earth parched to the pallor of bones – to the convent of the Incarnation, brown as cinnamon with its belfry and great buttresses, and garden walls sweeping back on either side, like the wings of a bird.

Heat of this intensity annuls time. You find yourself back in Teresa's century. Or, rather, has she stepped forward into ours?

I have been in many convents founded by Teresa. Yet in none of them, not even in the first foundation, St Joseph's in Ávila, does her spirit live as it does in the convent of the Incarnation, where she entered the religious life. Possibly this is because, in founding the numerous Discalced convents, as they came to be called, Teresa, whatever the practical difficulties (and they were considerable), knew precisely what she had in mind to do. During the years in the Incarnation, on the other hand, she was a learner, a beginner, struggling to find her feet. In retrospect this was seen as a time of waiting : waiting upon the will of God which became clear to her only gradually – a time of set-backs, doubts, disappointment. At one moment the religious life delighted her. At the next she was downcast and bored. In chapel, when she should have been praying, she was watching the hands of the clock go round. To have to intone an antiphon embarrassed her. She did not like to make a fool of herself : she had little ear for music, and, furthermore, did not always bother to practise. Whereas, unlike some of the sisters, she did not, she says, talk to people through crevices or over walls – nor have conversations in the night – yet in what she calls 'this hurly-burly of a place' she was not all she should have been. Only gradually, as the years slipped by, did the Divine Potter mould his clay to his purpose.

When Teresa entered the Incarnation there were no less than a hundred and fifty nuns there. Among them, as in other religious houses, were those who had nowhere else to take themselves. Some had been left widows, others were unmarried because their fathers could not provide adequate dowries. There were those, too, who had been unfortunate in a love-affair.

Life in the convent was not strict. Nuns were allowed to be away on long visits. Indeed this was encouraged because it saved the expenses of the community, who sometimes had not enough to eat. At one time, Teresa writes, she was hardly ever in the convent – intelligent and gay, she was much in demand. And when she was in the Incarnation, she enjoyed the privilege, because she was well provided for by her father, of a spacious cell and off it a kitchen and guest room. She used to have her sister to stay. Furthermore there was an interminable coming and going of visitors in the *locutorio* or parlour, which was a kind of salon, where conversation ranged over music, literature and the iniquities of the Lutherans. Young gallants, staring wistfully through the grille, would slip in gifts of candied fruits, sweet potatoes and other delicacies from the New World.

A life of this kind could not satisfy a woman of Teresa's latent spirituality, intelligence, and enterprise. Hence in 1562, accompanied by a small group of friends, she left the Incarnation to found, in Ávila, St Joseph's, the first convent of what came to be called the Reform. She was to found in all seventeen convents, as well as being instrumental in founding at Duruelo the first monastery of Discalced Friars.

On her way from the Incarnation to St Joseph's, Teresa, tradition tells, went barefoot into the crypt of the church of San Vicente where she prayed before the candlelit shrine of *La Virgen de La Soterrana*. From that time she ceased to be Doña Teresa de Cepeda y Ahumada. Instead, she was Teresa de Jesús.

Teresa was forty-three when the idea of the Reform came to her during a conversation which took place in her cell at the Incarnation. At first she did not consider the enterprise very seriously. Then gradually she realised that this was the work to which she was called: her shallow way of life must be abandoned. The convent she visualised would be one where persons so disposed could live in accordance with the Primitive Rule of the Carmelites as drawn up by Fray Hugo, Cardinal of Santa Sabina in the year 1348, before it was mitigated by Pope Eugenius in 1443.

With this in mind Teresa managed to buy a small, shabby house. Her intention was that the life should be simple, lived in the spirit of the original hermits of Mount Carmel, consecrated to silence and contemplative prayer. It would be no sense, she remarks tartly, if on the day of judgment a huge ornate building were to come crashing down on thirteen nuns – the number signifying Christ and his Apostles. St Joseph would keep watch at one door, Our Lady at the other. From it would shine forth a light as of a star: *sería una estrella que diese de sí gran resplandor.*

Despite opposition from religious and laity who complained (not without reason) that there were already too many convents in Ávila, St Joseph was founded. The five years spent in it were, Teresa says, the happiest in her life. This, however, could not last. Other convents were waiting to be founded.

In 1568 she and some companions were on the move, travelling in a mule cart to Medina del Campo. In the *Foundations* – a most entertaining travel book – she tells how on the outskirts of Medina they got down from the carts, went the rest of the way on foot, to avoid attracting attention, for it was the hour at which the bulls were enclosed for the fight on the next day. Laden with vestments and other requirements for saying Mass, they looked like a pack of gypsies who had robbed a church. The rest of the night was passed in scrubbing, sweeping, and hammering nails into the walls of the dilapidated house which was all they could acquire.

This, roughly, was the pattern of Teresa's life until she died some twenty years later.

It has been held against her that she was always on the go : that she founded convents where a life of strict enclosure was observed, yet, apart from a few brief periods, did not live this life herself. For, as well as travelling, she associated with persons of every rank from King Philip II and the Duke and Duchess of Alba to the humblest muleteer.

If, however, it be accepted that convents of enclosed nuns are a necessary component of the Church (and this is not the place to weigh the issue) it is hard to see how she could have done otherwise. It was essential that she should make the foundations in person and be available to help resolve problems that arose from convent to convent. More interesting is the fact that this nun, dedicated to silence and contemplation, lived, as it turned out, a life of exceptional activity. The interest is the greater because even a cursory reading of her works reveals a woman who, had she been confined year in and year out within the walls of a convent, would almost certainly have become, from sheer frustration, a victim of what in her day was called melancholia, in our own, mental illness.

The journeys were indeed formidable. The roads, at best tracks following the contours of the mountains, were beset by robbers or made impassable by snow, ice, or floods. Moreover, fastidious to a degree unusual in her times, Teresa nevertheless endured verminous inns crowded with picadors and soldiers. To avoid inns she sometimes slept out of doors. At Córdoba, before taking a siesta, she had to chase away pigs from under the Roman bridge.

And it was not only the hardships entailed on the

journeys. The end of each brought its own problems. At Salamanca she had to spend the vigil of All Souls locked in a room in a house recently vacated by students (and a fine mess they left behind!) in the company of a nun who could talk of nothing but the possibility of imminent death, while out in the streets the bells tolled. At Seville there were no bedclothes and not a soul to bring so much as a jug of water. At Segovia she was met by a Vicar-General who, because she had come with a verbal not a written permit, flew into such a towering rage that Julián de Ávila, a priest who had accompanied her, took refuge behind a staircase.

Throughout her life Teresa had to put up with dis-approval. In Ávila she heard herself denounced from the pulpit by a preacher ranting about nuns who left the enclosure of their convent. Her sister looked at her in concern, only to see her 'having a quiet laugh'. Warned that she might be summoned before the Inquisitors, Teresa again laughed, saying that if she saw any likelihood she would forestall this by visiting them herself. When she left Ávila for Medina del Campo in 1567 people said she was mad. Fourteen years later the Papal Nuncio described her as 'a restless, disobedient, contumacious gad-about, who under the cloak of piety had invented false doctrines . . . and gone about teaching, contrary to the injunctions of St Paul'.

Teresa of Ávila was not only a reformer and a pioneer. She was one of the world's great mystics, and much of her writing, though by no means all, is concerned with her own experiences, as well as mysticism in general. A Dominican contemporary Padre Pedro Ibáñez, who esteemed her highly, confessed that in reading the *Life* he found too much about visions and the like.

All her readers are not mystics, nor do they necessarily

think in terms of 'intellectual visions', 'the prayer of union', 'the prayer of recollection', 'the prayer of quiet', and so on. But Teresa did not intend that undue importance should be attached to these 'labels'. Again and again she emphasises that prayer cannot be divided into rigid compartments. In the *Interior Castle* she says that we must not imagine there are only the seven mansions of which she speaks – there are thousands.

It was the excellence of Teresa's teaching on prayer at every level that led Pope Paul VI to proclaim her a Doctor of the Church (15 October, 1967), thus raising her to the status of such giants in the spiritual life as her contemporary St John of the Cross, St Francis of Sales (1567–1622), and St Alphonsus Liguori (1696–1787).

'From foolish devotions may God defend us', she says. And why, she asks, pile up a multiplicity of words when the seven petitions contained in the *Our Father* cover all our needs, spiritual and temporal? Basically, then, Teresa's teaching is not only theologically sound, it is simple. A reader, however coming to her works for the first time must be prepared (and this calls for courage and perseverance) to distinguish what is fundamental from the extraneous. For whatever help or consolation Teresa derived from visions or the like, she was at one with St John of the Cross in believing that these phenomena are no guarantee of union with God or of genuine goodness. Again and again she questioned their validity and accepted her confessor's verdict even when it conflicted with her own convictions. Nevertheless it must be admitted that she evaluated her own mystical experiences with a seriousness she did not always concede to those of others. Of one of her nuns she said: 'If I'd been there she wouldn't have had such a whirl of experiences.'

What would Teresa's attitude have been towards

what we speak of today as charismatic renewal? She was without the inhibitions which make it hard for some to participate in charismatic prayer groups. Moreover she realised the necessity for orderliness and discipline – a need emphasised by Pope Paul when expressing his appreciation of charismatics during a congress held in Rome in 1973. Finally, Teresa again and again dwells on the supreme importance of a personal relationship between Christ and each one of us and this, it could be said, is the overriding aim of charismatic renewal.

In Teresa's view prayer is not a pious practice. It is an attitude to life; more than that, it is a way of life. And, to live this life, the will is all-important. If there is the will to pray, the will to love – if the will is orientated towards God, it is possible (no matter how great our turmoil of spirit) to find, on a level untouched by the senses, a pool of tranquillity. God is not 'up there' or 'out there'. He dwells within each of us : a *deus absconditus.* We have no need to ascend to him, no need to speak in a loud voice. Each one of us has only to withdraw within ourselves, like a tortoise or a hedgehog.

This might give the impresssion that Teresa thinks of prayer as a turning of one's back on the world. This is not so. The soul which she describes as having soared aloft to God remains tethered to earth as if by a thread of such delicacy that it is not felt as a hindrance – of such strength that it cannot be severed. For Teresa, prayer does not become a vague intoxicant as it did for her contemporaries the *Alumbrados* or *Illuminati* who regarded prayer as being so remote from the material world that to meditate even on Christ in his humanity was a barrier to perfect contemplation. As Teresa sees it, there is no rigid 'either – or' dividing the spiritual from the material : contemplative prayer is not inseparable from activity.

In the *Interior Castle,* when the soul has reached the Seventh Mansion where it is granted a foretaste of the Beatific Vision, it must of necessity drop back to earth to busy itself in the service of mankind. Did Paul, she asks, shut himself up with his visions, enjoying spiritual consolations? Not at all! Did the woman of Samaria, to whom Christ spoke at Jacob's well, spend her life thereafter dreaming her days away? Quite the contrary. Nor is Teresa ashamed to admit to her brother Lorenzo that sheer pressure of work has made prayer, in the formal sense, impossible.

Christ the Word made flesh is, for Teresa, both the pivot and the goal of prayer. All that matters is that we keep our eyes on Christ. She speaks of seeing him in visions, especially in the glory of his resurrected body. But she does not need a vision to make her aware of his presence. Asked by her bewildered confessor how she can know that Christ is at her side – since she cannot see him nor hear him nor is there anyone at hand to assure her he is there – she can only reply that she knows this with a greater certainty than could come through any of the senses.

*

A pleasing trait in Teresa is her openness – her lack of self-conscious attempts to 'edify'.

To a cleric she writes: 'Father, it is not at all necessary to swear – still less like a muleteer.' And to the grim Philip II: 'Remember, Sire, Saul was anointed, yet he was rejected.' Nor has she illusions as to the failings to which religious are especially prone. Indeed, she has much to say about nuns who take affront if not addressed with the reverence to which they consider themselves entitled – about prioresses who misuse their authority. Nor does she regard the laity as 'second-class citizens'. What matters,

24

she says, is not whether we wear the religious habit but whether our lives are truly Christian. One of the persons whose advice she most valued at a time of spiritual crisis was a married man: a citizen of Ávila – *uno caballero santo*.

Teresa transcends her times, but she is also a product of them. It is not surprising, therefore, to find her believing that the Lutherans are *ipso facto* incorrigibly wicked; that the devil is busy stoking up a hell-fire that is a literal reality. She is deeply concerned that in the New World thousands of souls are being lost – but, as Fr Anselm, o.d.c.* has observed with discernment, it is not clear whose these souls are – the natives to whom the Gospel had not been preached or 'the *conquistadores* who were more busy with plunder and exploitation than with spiritual concerns.' Indeed the surprising thing about St Teresa is not the degree to which her outlook conforms with that of sixteenth-century Spain, but rather her capacity to transcend a period when fanaticism exaggerated penances and, in general, a negative, intolerant attitude were the order of the day. Again and again she advocates discretion and common sense.

The secret of the spiritual life, as she understands it, is 'to flee from all to the All'. But this is an attitude of mind, not a rule to be carried out to the letter. She is not impressed by the suggestion of her brother Lorenzo that he should get rid of his carpets, so as to live in greater austerity. Moreover, the Rule she drew up to be observed by the convents of the Reform was intended as a framework within which the spiritual life might be led in community: a defence against the whims of intransigent

St Teresa of Ávila, edited by Fr Thomas and Fr Gabriel, o.d.c., Clonmore and Reynolds 1967.

Superiors : a code deserving of respect not on its own account but for the sake of those for whom it was made : a means to an end, not an end in itself. With characteristic good sense, she says that our nature should not be subjected to undue constraint. Men of talent (she particularly wanted to bring these into the Order) would be frightened off by an excess of austerity. The Lord, she says, has led her by love. And this, she concludes, must apply to others besides herself.

Pope John XXIII was sorely tried by 'prophets of doom', always foretelling disaster. Indeed it is true that the devout can appear at times to take pleasure in being gloomy. This needs to be stressed, for a sentence picked out of Teresa's writings here or there could convey the opposite impression. She speaks of herself as 'a miserable worm', 'the worst of sinners', 'a poor foolish woman' – it was the jargon of the day. But on balance her writings give quite another impression.

Gaiety and humour colour her letters. Asking her brother Lorenzo to send her seal stamped with the letters I.H.S., she adds : 'I can't endure sealing my letters with this death's head I'm now using.' To the Prioress at Seville who expected a visit from some Jesuits she writes : 'Think out questions to ask them. That's what they like.' And to Padre Gracián : 'How you made us laugh about the food in the hospital. Those ghastly cod patties !'

From her letters and her formal writings emerges a woman who had not only trust in the infinite goodness of God but a zest for life. One need only read in the *Foundations* about her encounter in a church at Toledo with a flashly dressed young gallant (not at all the type of person, she says, for Discalced Carmelites to be seen talking to), who, having promised to find the nuns somewhere to live, returned the following morning, a bunch of keys in his hand, to say that a house was at their disposal.

Again, she writes humorously of the convent at Pastrana, founded thanks to the generosity of the Prince and Princess of Éboli. As long as the Prince was alive all was well, apart from a certain amount of interference on the part of his wife whom Teresa manipulated with a skilful firmness coupled with tact. When, however, the Prince suddenly died it was another matter. Without more ado the Princess decided to become a nun. Whereupon she drove up to the convent with her luggage and two maids in attendance. 'We're finished!' the Prioress exclaimed in horror. She was right. The Princess, after two days of exaggerated humility, showed herself in her true colours. She expected to be treated in a manner befitting her rank – even requiring the nuns to wait on her on their knees.

Teresa promptly arranged for the community to move to the convent she had founded at Segovia – giving strict injunctions to the nuns to take with them nothing that had been given by the Princess or her late husband. The precaution was a wise one, for hardly had the nuns settled at Segovia when they were threatened with a lawsuit.

The journey to Segovia deserves mention. At dead of night they left Pastrana, making their way on foot to the top of a hill, where Julián de Ávila awaited them with five waggons. The next day there was trouble crossing a river by means of a ford. The waggons had scarcely entered the water in single file when those in front were caught in a current. The mules stopped dead, refusing to go backwards or forwards. There was a terrific uproar – Julián de Ávila calling to the muleteers, the muleteers to the animals, and the nuns to God.

Teresa's last foundation was at Burgos. And the journey the most difficult of all. She was unwell when she left Ávila at the beginning of January 1582, accompanied by Padre Gracián, her confessor, two friars, and three nuns. All the way to Medina del Campo there was rain and snow. At Valladolid, Teresa developed a throat infection. From there they pushed on to Valencia, where the crowds thronged around the mule carts, eager to catch a glimpse of Teresa, to ask a blessing from this woman who, rumour ran, was a 'saint'.

Worse was to come. So bad were the floods, that the friars had to keep going ahead to find the road. At the ford outside Burgos the water had risen to such a height that the bridges across the river were no longer visible. The party made their confession in readiness for death, then recited the creed. Teresa, urging her nuns to be prepared to die for Christ, went ahead in the first cart that entered the water. She told her companions that, were she to be drowned, they should return to the inn where they had spent the previous night.

They were at last nearing their destination when Padre Gracián, whose common sense did not match his piety, persisted that before going to the home of the lady in Burgos who was to be their hostess they should visit the *Cristo de Burgos,* then in the Augustinian church outside the city, now in the cathedral. This crucifix is indeed remarkable. With its human hair, its emaciated body draped in a crimson skirt, it has a strange primitive quality – as though this Christ had taken upon himself the unspoken terrors of primeval man : as though he were paying the price for blood shed on pagan altars and in secret groves.

The following day Teresa was so ill that she could not lift her head from the pillow. Nor did her troubles end there. The Archbishop of Burgos proceeded to oppose the foundation she had come to make. She better go back to Ávila, he told her. 'And the weather so charming!' Teresa commented. It was indeed strange, she reflected, that his Grace was unaware, apparently, of the inconvenience he was causing. Beyond this, not a word of criticism passed her lips, with the consequence that before many weeks had passed the Archbishop acceded to her wishes. More than that, he publicly expressed his regret for the delay he had caused – as well as his admiration and affection for Teresa.

Early in September Teresa, accompanied by one of her nuns, Ana de San Bartolomé,' set out for Ávila, travelling south over vast distances of plain with its stubble and ochre earth, poplar trees, and flat-topped hills, their ashen pallor refracting the crimson and gold of evening skies. She was exhausted and unwell. But she would rest, she told herself, at the convent at Medina del Campo before continuing to Ávila. This, however, was not to be. At Medina she received an urgent summons from the Duchess of Alba, asking that Teresa should make a detour by way of Alba de Tormes so as to be with her daughter-in-law who was expecting to give birth to a child. The Duchess had sent a coach to avoid delay.

It is a long, desolate road from Medina to Alba de Tormes. And Teresa was ill – so ill that Ana de San Bartolomé thought she was going to die. They could not get so much as an egg to eat – only dried figs and on the next day cabbage cooked in onion. They were nearing Alba de Tormes when they were met with the news that the Duchess of Alba's daughter-in-law had been delivered of a child. 'So the "saint" won't be needed', was Teresa's caustic retort, after which she asked to be taken not to the ducal castle but to the convent in Alba de Tormes which she had herself founded.

Teresa had a particular affection for Alba de Tormes. From her cell she could see the river that, slipping under the many-arched Roman bridge, reflects poplar trees by day, stars by night. She had always liked water. 'What would become of us without water?' she exclaims in the *Ways of Perfection*. Water was useful, beautiful, and mysterious. Again and again in her spiritual writing it is the symbol of God's grace. The mere sight of it gave her pleasure. Recalling a journey from Valencia to Soria she says it was a *recreación* because all the way she had glimpses of the river to keep her company.

Teresa died at Alba de Tormes on 4 October 1582. Ávila was in her thoughts. A short while before her death she said to Ana de San Bartolomé: 'As soon as I am better get me a cart, and we'll go to Ávila.' *Vamos a Ávila.*

*

Today Teresa lives for us in her writings: her letters and her formal works, in particular the *Life*, the *Way of Perfection*, the *Interior Castle*, and the *Foundations*. Regrettably we cannot read her commentary on the *Song of Songs*: she destroyed it to satisfy her confessor who had no fault to find with the writing – only with the fact that it had been written by a woman. No wonder she used to say that to be a woman was 'to feel your wings droop'.

It has been objected that being a woman she does not write with the logicality of her fellow countryman, St John of the Cross. How could she? Unlike him, she was not educated by Jesuits nor in the University of Salamanca. Indeed she had practically no education as we understand the word today. Nevertheless, despite digressions, repetitions, colourful but sometimes confused imagery, a thread of logic runs through her works, making it possible to assess with clarity her basic teaching on prayer – indeed to follow this step by step.

Too much is sometimes made of the fact that she wrote under obedience. Pressed for time and suffering from noises in the head, she asks to be left alone to get on with her spinning. Nevertheless she was a born writer of the highest calibre. The fact that today she is more popular in her own country than any writer other than Cervantes – that she is read the world over by Catholics, Calvinists, Orthodox, Buddhists, and Hindus – this speaks for itself.

And this is because her writing, apart from the teaching it contains, has remarkable charm. Particularly charming, and characteristic of a woman's writing at its best is her lightness of touch, her love of nature, her observation of detail, her ability to sum up a human being in a few telling phrases. It would be wrong, too, to suppose that she was indifferent to the niceties of style. Comparing the *Interior Castle* to the *Life* she says : 'It is composed of finer enamel and more precious metals; the goldsmith was less skilful when he made the first.'

PART TWO

From the writings of Teresa of Ávila

ABBREVIATIONS

L. – Life
W.P. – Way of Perfection
I.C. – Interior Castle
F. – Foundations
S.R. – Spiritual Relations
M. – Maxims
V.C. – Visitation of Convents
C.L.G. – Conceptions of Love of God

I. SERVANTS OF LOVE

I shall now say something of those who are beginning to become servants of Love – for this, I believe, is what we become when we determine to follow along this path of prayer him who has proved his great love of us. Merely to think about the honour he does us is a solace hard to put into words. Servile fear at once vanishes.

L. XI

Our goodness derives not from our capacity to think but to love.

F. V

Do whatever, therefore, most encourages you to love. Perhaps we do not know what love is? It would not surprise me to learn that this were so, for love depends not on the degree of our happiness but on our determination to please God in all things.

I.C. IV i

Do not imagine that one should never think of anything else – that if your mind wanders all is lost!

ibid.

Love begets love

Whenever we think of Christ let us remember the love wherewith he has showered upon us so many blessings – how great the love God has revealed in granting this pledge of the love he bears us. For love begets love. We may be only beginners. We may be evil. Even so let us remember God's love for us and awaken in us our own love, for if God in his mercy implants this love in our hearts, all will be easy for us and we shall get things done in a short time with little effort. May God grant us this love! He knows how much we need it for the sake of the love which he bore us and revealed to us in his Son who proved it at such cost to himself.

L. XXII

Fix your eyes on the Lord

Fix your eyes on the Lord who was crucified. Then nothing else will greatly matter to you. If he has revealed his love for us by behaving and suffering in a manner that seems beyond our comprehension, how can you suppose you will please him with words alone? Persons who are truly spiritual, let me tell you, have become the slaves of God. They are branded with his sign, the sign of the Cross, thus showing they have surrendered their freedom to him. He can then sell them to be slaves to the entire world, as was he himself. In doing this he will do them no wrong – rather he will confer no small favour.

Therefore, if you want to lay firm foundations, you must try, each one of you, to be the least of all, the slave of God. And this entails finding ways and means to please and to serve your companions without distinction.

I.C. VII iv

I would never want the kind of prayer that does not make the virtues grow within us. If with my prayer there are strong temptations and periods of aridity and tribulation and these make me more humble, that I would call good prayer – for the best prayer is the kind most pleasing to God. Nor must we conclude that a person who is suffering is not praying. He is offering his sufferings to God and is often praying with deeper sincerity than someone who goes away in a corner and meditates his head off and, if he squeezes out a few tears, imagines that is prayer!

To P. Jerónimo Gracián, Seville;
from Toledo, October, 1576

Even at times of illness or other afflictions we can still pray in the real sense of the word, provided there is love in the soul. We can offer to God whatever our affliction may be, remembering him for whose sake we are suffering this, as well as the thousand other things that may befall us. It is here that love comes in; for we are not necessarily praying when we are alone nor need we refrain from prayer when we are not alone.

L. VII

He held me in his hand

I suffered great affliction when I tried to pray, for my spirit instead of being master was slave. I was unable, therefore, to shut myself within myself (and this is my entire way of prayer, without at the same time shutting in a thousand irrelevancies. I passed many years like this. Indeed, when I look back, I am astonished that anyone could have gone on so long without abandoning one way or another. But I realised that by this time it was no longer possible to give up prayer; he who desired me for himself, to bestow his blessings upon me, held me in his hand.

L. VII

During these many years, except after receiving Communion, I did not dare to begin to pray without a book. I was scared to do so – as though I were going to fight against a host of enemies. A book gave me confidence: it was, so to speak, a companion, or a shield with which to parry the blows dealt by my thoughts.

L. IV

I had such difficulty in picturing things in my mind that if I did not actually see something I could not do so – as many can – with my imagination and thus become recollected. I could *think* of Christ as Man, but, however much I read about his beauty, however often I looked at pictures, I could not visualise him myself. I was like one who is blind or in the dark; he may be talking to someone else, know with certainty that the person is there; that is to say, he understands and believes the other is present, yet cannot see him.

L. IX

Boredom and a remedy

Often, for several years on end, I was more taken up with wishing away my hour of prayer and listening whenever the clock struck, than in thinking good thoughts. Again and again I would have chosen any severe penance that might be imposed on me rather than have to practise recollection as a preparation to prayer. For either in consequence of the overwhelming power of the devil's assaults or my own bad habits, I was not able to pray at once. Indeed when I went into the oratory I used to feel so depressed that I had to summon up all my courage to be able to pray at all. Afterwards, however, when I had forced myself to pray, I experienced a greater sense of serenity and happiness than when, at other times, I had prayed because I chose to.

L. VIII

It used to help me to look at a field or water or flowers. They reminded me of my Creator.

L. IX

A storm-tossed sea

I passed almost twenty years on this storm-tossed sea, now engulfed in the waters, now rising again, but only to be engulfed once more.

L. VIII

This, I assure you, is a most grievous state of affairs, for I found neither joy in God nor satisfaction in the world. When I was caught up in the pleasures of the world I was unhappy in recalling what I owed to God. When I was with God I was restless, craving for what the world had to offer. So distressing was this conflict of mind that I do not know how I endured it for a month, let alone for many years. And yet I realised the greatness of God's compassion for me, for while I was still entangled with the affairs of the world he gave me the courage to pray.

ibid.

God within us

This was my way of prayer. As I could not reason things out, I tried to picture Christ within. Moreover, I got on better when I concentrated most on the many occasions in his life when he was alone. The fact that he was alone and in distress made it easier to approach him. I was particularly drawn to his prayer in the garden of Gethsemane. I used to go there, so to speak, to keep him company. I used to think of the sweat and the sorrow he endured. I would have liked to wipe the sweat from his face, but I did not dare to make such a resolve : my sins stood in my way.

L. IX

For many years (this was before I became a nun) on most nights before falling asleep I used to think for a while about the prayer in the garden. This, I believe, did me good, for, without knowing it, I was learning how to pray. And because I had become used to this I did not abandon it – just as I never gave up the habit of making the sign of the Cross before falling asleep.

ibid.

Remember what St Augustine tells us – how he sought God in many places, then found him within himself. However softly we speak, God will hear us. We need no wings to soar in search of him : he is within us.

W.P. XXVIII

Those of us who can shut ourselves up in this little heaven of the soul where dwells the Creator of heaven and earth will, without fail, drink of the water of Life.

We will journey a long way in a short time – like a traveller on board ship who, if he has a good wind, reaches his destination in a few days.

ibid.

There is no need to raise our voices. He himself will reveal to us that he is there and so we will be able to say the *Our Father*, or any prayer we like, with tranquillity of mind.

W.P. XXXIX

I have sometimes experienced a sudden awareness of God so strong that I had no doubt whatever that he was within me and I wholly engulfed in him.

L. X

I realised one day that God is in all things – that he is within the soul. I recalled how a sponge absorbs water.

S. R. XLV

The Lord, without the need of any door, will come into the centre of the soul – as when he came to his disciples and said to them : 'Peace be to you', and when he left the tomb without removing the stone.

I.C. VI

Do not suppose that the understanding can comprehend God simply by trying to think of him as being within the soul or by picturing him with the imagination. This, indeed, is a good thing to do, an excellent form of meditation, for it is founded on a truth – namely that God is within us. But this is not the kind of prayer I have in mind, for anyone (with God's help, that is) can practise this for himself. I am describing something different. I am thinking of those who suddenly find themselves in the King's castle before they are aware of God at all. I cannot say where they entered or how they came to hear the Shepherd's pipe – it was not with their ears, for this call is not audible. No, they become more and more aware that they are gradually withdrawing into themselves. I cannot put it better, but anyone who has experienced this will know what I mean. I have read, I think, that there is a resemblance here to a hedgehog or a tortoise. Yet it is not quite the same. These creatures withdraw into themselves whenever they like. With us it is not a question of the will. It happens only when it is God's pleasure.

I. C. III iii

No one who has begun to pray, no matter how many sins he may commit, should ever abandon this practice. For it is by prayer that we can amend our lives : without prayer this will be much more difficult.

L. VIII

And anyone who has not begun to pray, I beg him for the love of God not to miss so great a blessing. Even if he makes no progress – even if he does not strive after perfection so as to enjoy the consolations and the blessings given by God to the perfect – he will gradually learn about the road that leads to heaven, if he perseveres; his hope I believe, is in the mercy of God whom no one has taken as a friend without being thankful for it. For mental prayer is, in my opinion, nothing other than a loving relationship and a frequent solitary conversation with him who we know loves us.

ibid.

Although we are always in God's presence, this is true in a special way, I believe, when we are praying. For then we are aware that God is looking at us, whereas at other times we might be in his presence for several days, yet not remember that he sees us.

L. VIII

Vocal and mental prayer

Do you imagine that God is silent because we cannot hear him? He speaks directly to our hearts when, from our hearts, we ask him to do so. It is a good idea to imagine that God has taught the Lord's prayer to each one of us individually and that he is continually revealing its meaning more and more to us. The Master is never far away; his disciple need not speak loudly to be heard. Please understand that, if you are to say the *Our Father* well, this one thing is necessary : that you do not leave the side of him who has taught it.

You will reply that this is meditation and that you cannot meditate and do not even want to try – that you are content with vocal prayer. For there are people so impatient that they will not put themselves to the slightest trouble, and at first it is troublesome to recollect the mind when they are not used to it. Rather than exhaust themselves they say they are incapable of anything except vocal prayer and cannot do anything beyond this. You are, of course, right in saying that what I have spoken about is mental prayer. But I assure you I cannot distinguish this from vocal prayer faithfully recited with the realisation of whom we are addressing. God grant that we may say the *Our Father* well. For in my opinion this is necessary not just for nuns but for all who would pray as true Christians.

W. P. XXIV

As unruly as wild horses

There are those whose souls and minds are as unruly as wild horses. No one can control them. Now they dash in this direction, now in that.

W. P. XIX

They cannot recollect themselves or tie down their minds to mental prayer or to making a meditation. We must not speak of either – they will not hear of such things! Indeed, many appear to be terrified at the very mention of contemplation or mental prayer!

W.P. XXIV

In case any such person should come here (for, as I

have said, all are not led by the same road) I want to say something about how to practise vocal prayer, for it is right that you should understand what you are saying. Someone who is unable to think of God may be wearied by long prayers, so I shall speak only of prayers which, as Christians, we must of necessity recite: the *Our Father* and then *Hail Mary* – then it cannot be said we are repeating words without understanding what they mean. We may, it is true, think it enough to pray merely from habit – to repeat the words and think this is enough! But I should prefer not to be satisfied simply with that. When I say the Creed it is right, if not obligatory, to know what it is I believe; and when I say the *Our Father* love requires that I know who this Father is, and who the Master is who taught this prayer.

ibid.

Perseverance

For years I was unable to concentrate, and a sore affliction it is. But God does not leave us without help if we approach him humbly. If a whole year passes without our receiving what we ask we should be ready to try longer. Such time is well spent. This I am sure is a habit we can form and thus strive to walk alongside our Master.

I.C. XXI

Living water

He who wants to learn how to pray should imagine that he is going to make a garden in which the Lord will find pleasure – and this in a place where the soil is barren and weeds grow in plenty. Now it is the Lord himself who plucks up the weeds and puts good plants instead. Let us imagine, then, that this has been done – that the soul has resolved to devote itself to prayer and has already begun to do so. It is for us, by God's grace like good gardeners to make these plants grow. We must water them carefully so that they may not wither but bear blossoms that will give forth a fragrance pleasing to our Master so that he will visit the garden and take his pleasure among the flowers.

Let us now reflect how to water the garden, so that we may know what we have to do, what labour is involved, and how much time it will take. The garden, it seems to me, can be watered in four ways: first, by drawing the water from the well, at the cost of heavy labour; secondly by using a water-wheel and buckets, when the water is drawn by a windlass (I have done this myself sometimes; and it brings more water with less fatigue); thirdly by a stream or brook which is better still, for the soil is thoroughly saturated, the gardener's labours are less, and water is not needed so often; fourthly by a downpour of rain, and this last is far the best, for the Lord himself waters the garden without any aid from us.

L. XII

'I will give you to drink.' The Lord, remember, invites us all, and as he is Truth itself we cannot doubt his word. He might have said: 'Come all of you, for you have nothing to lose by coming, and I will give to drink those I think fit.' But as he made no such condition I am sure that no one will be debarred from receiving this living water unless they fail to keep to the path.

W. P. XIX

Yes, he calls us for all to hear, in a loud voice. Yet in his goodness he does not force us to drink. He enables those who want to follow him to drink in many ways so that none are at a disadvantage or left to die of thirst. For from this source of life flow many streams, some large, some small – there are even little pools for children who might be frightened by the sight of a great quantity of water. And so, I beg you, strive with all your might, confident that in this life you will have water from which you may drink and in the life to come a never-ending abundance.

W.P. XX

God does not lead us all along the same road

It is essential to realise that God does not lead us all along the same road. It may be that someone who thinks of herself as going along the lowliest road is the highest in the sight of the Lord. It does not follow, therefore, that, because we all in this convent practise prayer, we are of necessity contemplatives. That, indeed, is impossible. Moreover those of us who are not contemplatives would become greatly discouraged if we did not grasp the truth; namely, that contemplation is something given to us by God; it is not necessary for salvation. God will not ask it of us before he gives us our reward; nor will anyone require it of us. We shall not fail to attain perfection provided we do what is asked of us – indeed our merit will be the greater because what we do will demand more effort: the Lord, in fact, will be treating us as being among those who are strong and will have in store for us all that we cannot enjoy here and now. We must not, then, become discouraged.

W.P. XVII

Sometimes the Lord takes a long time, and then all at once gives us what he has been giving to others over a period of many years.

ibid.

As for myself, I spent over fourteen years without being able to meditate except while reading. There are no doubt many such persons, and others who cannot meditate even after reading, but can recite vocal prayers only. Some find their thoughts wandering to such an extent that it is impossible for them to concentrate. So restless are they that if they try to keep their mind on God they are beleagured by a thousand vain distractions, scruples, doubts.

ibid.

I know a nun, an old woman who has lived a most holy and penitential life, who for many years has spent hour after hour in vocal prayer, but derives no help whatsoever from mental prayer. The most she can do is to concentrate on the words of her prayers as she says them. There must be many like her. If they are humble they will, I am sure, be none the worse off, but very much the same as others who have experienced all sorts of spiritual consolations. In a way such people are safer, for we do not know whether 'consolations' come from God or from the devil. And if they are not from God they are the more dangerous, since the main purpose of the devil on earth is to fill us with pride. If, however, they come from God there is no danger, for they bring humility.

ibid.

Courage

Another thing : if we believe that the Lord has given us a particular grace, we must understand that it is a blessing from him, but one which he may take away again – as indeed often happens in the workings of providence. Sometimes, for instance, I think I am greatly detached, and indeed when it comes to the test I am; yet at other times I find myself so attached to things which the day before I would have scorned that I scarcely know myself. Another time I have such courage that there is nothing from which I would shrink were it to serve the Lord, and when called upon to face such things I do not fail. And then the next day, I find I would not have the courage to kill an ant for God's sake, should anyone oppose me. Sometimes it seems to matter not at all if people speak ill of me and when the test comes I even enjoy it. And then comes a day when one word distresses me, and I long to be out of the world altogether, so tedious everything is. And I am not the only person to whom this can happen.

W.P. XXXVIII

Beware of certain forms of humility that the devil instills into us, making us full of anxiety about the gravity of our past sins.

W.P. XXXIX

From the first we should be resolute in prayer.
W.P. XXIII

When God has given us so much we should be resolute in making some return, however small. What wife, who has been given valuable jewels by her husband will not give him, so much as a ring – not because of its value (all she has is his) but as a symbol of love, a token that she is his until she dies.

ibid.

The devil fears resolute souls : he knows from experience that when he tries to tempt them, they are the winners, he the loser.

ibid.

A resolute person fights with greater courage. He knows that, come what may, he must not withdraw.
ibid.

Do not fear that the Lord who has called us to drink of the water of life will leave us to die of thirst. People are often timid : they have not yet learnt by experience the Lord's goodness to us, though they know of it by faith.

ibid.

If you truly surrender yourself to God, cease to be anxious; he hears your anxiety and will always bear it.

W.P. XXXIV

To grasp all is to lose all

Some, when they feel joy in prayer, are tempted to imagine that they can prolong this joy by their own efforts. It is an absurd idea. We can no more control this than we can make dawn break or evening come down. It is supernatural – quite outside our powers.

W.P. XXXI

If we try to grasp all, we lose all.

ibid.

Our Father

You must understand that you are doing far more by now and again repeating a single petition of the *Our Father* than were you to repeat the whole prayer many times in a hurry, not thinking what you were saying. He to whom you are praying is very near to you and cannot fail to hear you.

ibid.

The sublime perfection of this prayer that has come to us from the Gospels is something for which we should thank the Lord. So well did our Master compose it that each can use it in his own way.

W.P. XXXVII

In the *Our Father* the Lord has taught us the whole
method of prayer and contemplation from the very
beginning of mental prayer to that of Quiet and Union.

ibid.

I have wondered why God did not discourse on such
a sublime theme in greater detail, to enable us to understand. And then it occurred to me that as this prayer was
to be one all could use – everyone could interpret as he
thought best, ask for what he needed and derive
comfort in doing so – the Lord purposely left it open, to
cover all situations. Contemplatives who no longer desire
the things of the earth and persons especially devoted to
God can ask for heavenly favours. Those still living on
earth and having to conform to their state of life may ask
for what they need so as to maintain themselves and their
households (as is fitting and right) and for anything else
they feel they need.

ibid.

We can say this prayer once only, yet in such a way
that the Lord knows there is no guile in us and that we
shall do what we say. For the Lord wills that in our
dealings with him we should be always sincere and open,
not saying one thing but meaning another. If we do this
he will grant us more than we can ask.

ibid.

What to pray for?

Let us not pray for worldly things. It makes me laugh, and at the same time distresses me when I hear the things which people who come here ask us to pray for. We are to ask the Almighty to give them money to provide a regular income – it is a pity some of them do not beg God to give them the strength to trample such desires beneath their feet. Their intentions are good enough and I do as they ask because I see they are really devout people, though I do not myself believe God hears me when I ask for such things. The world has gone up in flames. Men are trying to condemn Christ once more, bringing, as it were, a thousand false witnesses against him. They would like to raze his Church to the ground. Are we, at such a critical time, to waste our efforts on things which, if God were to grant them, would perhaps bring one soul less to heaven? This is indeed no time to ask God for things of no import.

W.P. I

For preachers and theologians

Let us try so to live that our prayers be of avail to those servants of God, who at the cost of much toil, fortified by much learning and virtuous living, labour in the service of the Lord!

W.P. III

These preachers and theologians have to live among, and associate with, their fellow men, stay in grand houses and sometimes, outwardly, behave as those who dwell in such houses.

ibid.

Pray to God, all of you, for our Father-General who fell off his mule and broke his leg. I'm most upset about it – he is getting on in years.

To M. María de San José, Seville;
from Toledo, July 1576

Please God that the gentleman who has got married may improve in health. You must not be so lacking in faith. Prayer can do anything and the closeness of your relationship to him will mean a great deal. We, too, will contribute our 'mite'.

To Don Francisco de Salcedo, Ávila;
from Valladolid, September 1568

The weather has been shocking. Cold. Snow. Ice. I hope you are well, also your son-in-law. I commend myself to the prayers of you both. With my wretched health I need them when faced with my journeys on these roads.

To Don Alonso Álvarez Ramirez, Toledo;
from Valladolid, February 1569

God grant you don't forget me in your prayers! Then I can put up with anything!

To P. Antonio de Segura;
from Toledo, Lent 1570

2. OUR NEIGHBOUR

The Lord asks two things of us : love of God and love of
our neighbour. If we want to know whether we are
keeping these commandments we must discover, I believe,
whether we genuinely love our neighbour. For we cannot
be sure if we are loving God – though we may have good
reasons to think so – whereas we can know if we love our
neighbour. And the further advanced you are in this, the
greater will be your love for God. For God loves us so
dearly that he will recompense our love for our neighbour
by increasing the love we have for him – and this in countless ways.

I.C. V iii

I do not think we can have perfect love of our neighbour unless it has its roots in our love of God. Since this
is all important we must try to know ourselves better even
in very small matters. Think of the grandiose plans that
crowd into our minds during prayer – how we will do this
or that or the other for the good of our neighbour, if it
be only in the hope of saving a single soul. If later, however, our actions are not in keeping with these plans, we
have no grounds for supposing we would ever put them
into practice. And what I say of this applies also to
humility and the other virtues. The deceits of the devil

are horrific : he will run a thousand times round hell if by doing so he can convince us that we possess a single virtue which in fact we do not possess.

ibid.

When I see someone trying to work out what kind of prayer they are practising and are so engrossed in prayer that they are afraid, apparently, to move an inch or spare a moment's thought, for fear they be deprived to the slightest degree of the devotion they are enjoying. I realise how little they know about the road to union with God. They think that this is the whole thing. Well, it isn't. Not at all. What the Lord wants is works. If you see someone sick to whom you can bring help, don't imagine your devotions will suffer. Have compassion. If she is in pain try to share her pain. If need be, go without food that she may have yours.

I.C. V iii

Ask the Lord to give you this perfect love for others. Allow him to work within you. If you do your best to fulfil this in every way you can, he will give you more than you can desire. You must be prepared to do violence to your own will, so that another's will may be done, even if you have to forego your rights and forget your own good out of concern for others, no matter how much your physical powers may rebel. If the chance presents itself, try to shoulder some burden so as to relieve your neighbour. But don't have any illusions that this will cost you nothing or that you will find it all done for you ! Think at what cost to himself our Saviour died for us.

ibid.

56

Shortcomings

Let us take note of our own shortcomings and leave other
people's alone. Those who live carefully regulated lives
are disposed to be shocked at everything, whereas we could
well learn important lessons from the very persons who
shock us. Our outward comportment and behaviour is
perhaps superior to theirs, but even if this matters, it is
not what matters most. There is no reason to presume
that everyone should travel by the same path as ourselves.
What is more, we should not point out to others the
spiritual path when very likely we do not know what it is.

I.C. III ii

There are some who by nature are easily cast down
about matters of little concern. If you are not one of these
be sure to have compassion on those afflicted in this way.
It is only right to feel compassion for the needs of others.

W.P. VII

It is a test of love if we can put up with the shortcomings
of others and not be shocked. Then others will put up
with ours.

ibid.

If one of you is annoyed with another about some
word spoken in haste, this ought to be put right and you
should pray about it with sincerity.

ibid.

Fall in with the humour of those with whom you are talking. Be joyful with those who are joyful, sad with those who are sad. In short, be all things to all men, and so win them over.

M. 8

Think of yourself as the servant of all. Look for Christ the Lord in everyone. Then you will respect and revere everyone.

M. 25

Don't compare one person with another. Comparisons are loathsome.

M. 44

To love is all-important. There is nothing, however tedious, which cannot be borne with a light heart by those who love one another.

W.P. IV

I have learnt from my own experience and that of others that God's servants have helped me most in times of trouble. . . . Moreover you will find parents and brothers and sisters where you least expected to find them.

W.P. IX

Do not be excessively strict with yourself, for if you become timorous in spirit this will detract from the good that is in you and may lead to scrupulosity which hinders progress both in yourself and in others.

W.P. XLI

I'm really annoyed about those falls of yours. You

58

should be tied on to your mount, then you couldn't fall off. I can't imagine what sort of a mule you have or why you have to cover ten leagues in a day. That's suicidal on a pack-saddle. I am also anxious to know if it has occurred to you to wear more clothes, now that the weather is getting cold. Please God you have done yourself no injury! Since you are so concerned about the welfare of others, think how many would suffer if you were to ruin your health. For the love of God take care!

To P. Jerónimo Gracián;
from Seville October 1575

I wrote to you the other day telling you to take the little black girl without any hesitation – and her sister.

To M. María de San José, Seville;
from Toledo, July 1577

Someone who tries not to offend God and has entered the religious life may suppose that everything possible has been done. But you must understand that there are always a few worms which you do not see until, like the worm which gnawed through the ivy of Jonas, they tunnel their way through our good qualities. I am thinking, for instance, of self-love, self-esteem, censoriousness (even in small matters) in our relations with our neighbour; lack of charity and a failure to love others as we ought.

I.C. V iii

They forget themselves

Those whom the Lord has raised to a high degree of prayer think no longer of themselves and possible loss or gain. They think only of pleasing God. Now, as they know how greatly he loves his servants, they gladly lay aside their own pleasure and profit, so as to please him by serving others. They do this as well as they can, without, as I have said, taking into account whether they lose or gain – they have at heart their neighbours' good and nothing else. To give God greater pleasure they forget themselves for the sake of others and, if need be, will lay down their lives as did the martyrs.

C.L.G. VII

I notice that the further some persons (they are few), advance along the path of prayer and the more blessings they receive from God, the more attentive they are to the wants of their neighbours.

ibid.

I have, I think, much more compassion for the poor than I used to have. I am deeply sorry for them and want to help them. If I could follow my own impulse I would give them the clothes off my back. I feel no revulsion in mingling with them and touching them. This, I realise, is a grace given me by God. Formerly, though I gave alms for love of God, I had no natural compassion.

S.R. II

We must not construct towers that have no foundations. Nor forget that the Lord does not look so much at the magnitude of what we do as at the love with which we do it.

I.C. VII iv

If this is your goal, I repeat, you must not build solely on foundations of prayer and contemplation. Unless you strive after the virtues and put them into practice you will never grow to be more than dwarfs.

ibid.

We should desire to pray and engage in prayer not to give ourselves pleasure, but to gain strength to fit us for the service of others.

ibid.

'Peace, peace', the Lord said. He spoke these words many times to the Apostles. Believe me, if we do not have peace and work for peace in our home, we shall not find it in the homes of others.

I.C. II i

Perfection consists not in spiritual consolations but in an increase of love. On this too will depend our reward – as well as on the goodness and the truth shown forth in our actions.

I.C. III ii

The *bolilla** is for Pedro de Ahumado. He spends so much time in church that his hands must get frozen.

To Don Lorenzo de Cepeda
January 1577

*A little metal ball filled with hot water, to keep your hands warm.

3. COMMON SENSE

Christ in glory

Sometimes our temperament or some indisposition will
not allow us to meditate on the Passion : it is too
distressing. But what can stop us from being with Christ
in his resurrected body, since we have him so close to us
in the Blessed Sacrament where he is already glorified?
Here we do not see him exhausted and broken in body,
blood streaming, worn out by his journeying, persecuted
by those to whom he was doing good, no longer believed
in by the Apostles. It is true that we cannot always endure
to think of the afflictions he suffered. But in his glorified
body we can look upon him free from pain, radiant, before
he ascends into heaven.

L. XXII

As in this world so, too, in the spiritual world there are
changes in the weather. This is unavoidable. Don't be
worried : it's not your fault.

To Don Antonio Gaytán, Alba de Tormes;
from Valladolid, December 1574

You are very silly to keep worrying about perfection

and imagining you are taking too much care of yourself, when it is important you should keep well.

To M. María Bautista, Valladolid;
from Segovia, July 1574

What Father Fray Juan de Jesús says about my wanting the friars to go barefoot is ludicrous! It was I who always forbade Fray Antonio to do so. My wish and intention has been to attract men of real talent, but they would be put off by an excess of austerity. Some young friars have ridden by on donkeys. They were apparently going a short distance and might as well have walked on their feet! It certainly doesn't look well to see these young men barefoot, yet mounted on saddled mules. There's too much of this 'going barefoot'. The emphasis should be on virtue not austerity.

To P. Ambrosio Mariano de San Benito;
from Toledo December 1576

Your health would get worse not better, I think, if you were to have the period of relaxation you mention. I'm convinced of this. I know your temperament. Your craving for solitude is better for you than the solitude itself.

To M. María Bautista Valladolid;
from Segovia, 14 May 1574

We cannot speak to God and to the world at the same time. Yet this is what we are attempting to do when, while saying our prayers, we are listening to other people's conversation or letting our thoughts dwell on anything that comes to mind. There are, it is true, times when this cannot be helped – during periods of ill health (especially when someone is suffering from acute depression); or if our heads are tired and however hard we try we cannot concentrate; or when, for our own good, God allows his servants to be exposed for days on end to tempestuous storms.

W.P. XXIV

The nature of suffering of this kind shows that the victim is not to blame and therefore should not worry (that only makes things worse) or grow weary in trying to put sense into a mind which for the time being is incapable of any. Such a person should pray as best she can or, indeed, not pray at all. It is better for her to try to relax as though she were ill, or else busy herself with some useful activity.

ibid.

There are people who think that they will lose all devotion if they relax for a little.

L. XIII

And yet there are many occasions when it is fitting that we should have some recreation, so as to be stronger when we return to prayer.

ibid.

In everything we need discretion.

ibid.

We must, of course, have great confidence, for we should not cramp our good aspirations but rather believe that, with God's help, if we make a continual effort, we shall attain (though not at once perhaps) to that which many saints have reached through his favour – if they had not resolved to reach these heights they would never have done so.

ibid.

God loves and wants courageous souls.

ibid.

I am astonished at how much can be achieved if one has the courage to strive for great things. The soul may not have the strength to do this immediately, but if it once takes flight it will make excellent progress – even if, like an unfledged bird, it may grow tired and stop.

ibid.

I often used to recall St Paul's words that in God all things are possible. Since I could do nothing of myself this was a great encouragement to me. So were the words of St Augustine: 'Give me, Lord, what you command me and command me what is your will.' I used to think, too that St Peter lost nothing by throwing himself into the sea, even though, when he had done so, he was afraid.

ibid.

Don't imagine it is always the devil who hinders prayer. Sometimes our ability to pray is taken from us by God in his compassion. For reasons I haven't time to go into I would say it is almost as great a mercy when God takes away our ability to pray as it is to bestow this upon us. The prayer he grants you is incomparably more valuable than meditations on hell. Anyway you aren't capable of meditating on hell, even if you tried. But don't try. You have no need!

To Don Lorenzo de Cepeda, Ávila;
from Toledo, January 1577

It doesn't tire me to read your letters. They are a great comfort. It would also be a great comfort to me to write to you more often. But I simply can't – I've so much work to do. Even writing to you tonight has kept me from prayer. But I feel no scruples, I'm just sorry I haven't had time.

ibid.

I send the hair shirt. You may wear it two days a week, from the time you get up till you go to bed. You mustn't wear it while you're asleep. If it goes right round your waist put a strip of linen across your stomach, otherwise it will be harmful. If it affects the kidneys you mustn't wear the hair-shirt at all or use the discipline – it would do you great harm. God wants your health and obedience more than acts of penance.

ibid.

We do not observe the smallest details of our Rule. Silence, for example, cannot hurt anyone. Yet we have scarcely begun to imagine our heads are aching when we absent ourselves from choir, though to be there would not kill us. On one day we stay away because we had a headache a while ago; another time because our head has begun to ache again; and then on the three following days for fear it might ache once more!

W.P. X

If once the devil begins to make us nervous about our health we'll never get anywhere.

ibid.

Remember too, how many women – those of high rank, I happen to know – have serious ailments and much to put up with, yet cannot bring themselves to say a word to their husbands for fear of upsetting them.

In saying this I am not thinking of serious illnesses – high fevers and the like. Though even in regard to these I hope you will try to exercise some restraint and patience.

W.P. XI

You are very silly to keep worrying about perfection and imagining you are taking too much care of yourself. It is important you should keep well.

To M. María Bautista, Valladolid;
from Segovia, July 1574

We are not angels. We have bodies. To want to be angels here on earth is absurd – particularly if you are as much part of the earth as I am.

L. XXII

I was upset that Padre Gracián should have gone to the trouble of refuting those scandals that have spread abroad about us. They are utterly absurd. The best thing is to laugh and let people go on saying them.

To M. María de San José Seville;
from Toledo, February 1577

We must not worry ourselves to death if we cannot think a single good thought. We are unprofitable servants and must accept our limitations. It is God's will that we be like the little donkeys that draw the waterwheel I mentioned earlier. Their eyes are covered and they have no idea what they are doing. Yet these donkeys draw more water than can the gardener, despite all his efforts.

L. XXII

Get well again

As to what you call interior trials, the more you have the less notice you should take. They are clearly the outcome of an unstable imagination and a weak constitution. When the devil sees someone afflicted in this way, he makes his own small contribution. But don't be alarmed. St Paul tells us that God will not let us be tempted beyond our endurance. Get well again, please. And, for the love of God, eat enough. Don't be by yourself. Don't think too much. Be as occupied as much as possible. I only wish I were with you. It would do you good to hear a bit of entertaining chatter!

To M. María Bautista, Valladolid;
from Toledo, November 1576

Religious in authority must not expect other nuns to become like us at once. To expect this would be absurd. They should not rigidly enforce silence or object to things not in themselves sinful. To take this line with persons

accustomed to a different way of life can lead the latter
to commit sins instead of avoiding them.

To M. María de San José, Seville;
from Toledo, January 1577

Stop worrying!

You must not wear yourself out by trying to think too
much or to worry about meditation. I have told you over
and over again – if you have not forgotten what you should
do and how; if you do this and occupy yourself with the
praise of God, you are receiving a great blessing from
him. If you feel everyone should be giving praise to God,
that is a sign you are occupied with him. May God teach
you how to serve him – and me, too! For that is part of
the debt we owe him – and may he give us plenty to put
up with – if only fleas, hobgoblins and the roads along
which we have to travel.

To Don Antonio Gaytán, Alba de Tormes;
from Segovia, June 1574

Ignore that feeling of wanting to break off in the
middle of a prayer. Thank God that you have the wish to
pray. For that, you can be assured, comes from the will,
which loves to be with God. It is just depression that
weighs you down and gives you a feeling of constraint.
Try sometimes, when you feel depressed, to go some place
where you can see the sky and walk up and down for a
while. That won't interfere with your prayer. We must
accept our human frailty and not subject ourselves to
undue constraint.

To Don Teutonio de Braganza, Salamanca;
from Segovia, July 1574

4. THE DEVIL

Holy water

Long experience has taught me that there is nothing like holy water for putting devils to flight and preventing them from coming back. They also flee from the Cross, but they come back again. Holy water must have a special power.

L. XXXI

One night I thought the devils were stifling me. Then, after the nuns sprinkled plenty of holy water, I saw a great crowd of devils making off at a terrific pace, as though they were going to fling themselves down a steep slope. I see now that unless the Lord permits it, they cannot stir and so I have lost all fear of them.

ibid.

Once in the oratory, on the feast of All Souls, I had said a nocturn and was repeating some prayers – particularly devotional ones that we have in our office book – when the devil actually alighted on my book to stop me from finishing the prayer. I made the sign of the Cross and he went away. Then, when I began to pray again, he came back. He came back three times, I think.

It was only when I sprinkled him with holy water that I could finish the prayer.

ibid.

The devil has only to see a door ajar and in he comes to play countless tricks on us.

I.C. VI ix

A learned man used to say that the devil is a clever painter. Supposing, he continued, the devil were to show him a genuine likeness of the Lord, far from worrying, he would use Satan's own weapon to make war upon him. For however evil the painter, one cannot but revere the picture – if indeed it is a likeness of him who is our sole Good.

ibid.

The devil works like a noiseless file – so we must be on our guard from the very beginning. Let me be more explicit. He inspires, for instance, a sister with a passion for acts of penance, so that she has no peace of mind, it seems, unless she is torturing herself. And this when the prioress has said that acts of penance are not to be performed without permission ! And so the sister ruins her health and cannot do what her Rule requires. Another sister shows such zeal for perfection that trivial faults in others assume in her eyes exaggerated proportions, and she is always running with complaints to the prioress.

I.C. I ii

The devil under the guise of humility led me into the

greatest of all errors. I was so evil, I thought, that I was afraid to pray.

L. VII

For a year or more I did not pray, thinking that not to pray was a mark of greater humility. This was indeed the greatest temptation I had known : it nearly destroyed me.

ibid.

With the help of a cross I believed I could prevail over all devils. 'Come here now, the lot of you,' I said, 'I am a servant of the Lord and I want to see what you can do to me !'

L. XXV

So many flies

I lost all the fears that till then used to disturb me. Although I sometimes saw devils I was scarcely ever again afraid of them – on the contrary, they seemed afraid of me. I have acquired over them an authority conferred upon me by the Lord. They trouble me no more than so many flies.

ibid.

'The devil, the devil,' we say, when we could be saying 'God, God,' and make the devil shudder. Indeed, we could do so, for, as we know, Satan cannot lift a finger unless the Lord permits. Without a doubt I am more afraid of those who are frightened by the devil than I am of the devil himself !

ibid.

How many there are whom the devil has lead astray –
causing them to think their misgivings and other such
frailties stem from humility, whereas in reality they come
from a lack of self-knowledge. We get a distorted view of
our own nature, and, if we do not stop thinking about
ourselves, it is no wonder we experience these fears and
worse. We must keep our eyes fixed on Christ our sole
good, from whom we can learn real humility, as we can,
too, from his saints. Then our understanding will be
ennobled and our self-knowledge will not be of a kind to
make us timorous and full of fear. Terrible indeed are
the wiles of the devil by which we are hampered
from knowing ourselves and recognising his ways.

I.C. I ii

To disturb the soul and prevent it from enjoying the
blessings that come from God, the devil will suggest a
thousand groundless fears and cause others to do the
same.

W.P. XL

Things get into such a quandary that a person no
longer believes in the mercy of God and nothing she does
seems to be of any avail. And so she loses confidence and
sits, her hands in her lap, thinking she can do nothing
and that what is good in others is not good in her.

In contrast, true humility neither disquiets nor troubles
nor disturbs the soul. It is accompanied by peace, joy
and tranquillity. Far from having a depressing effect it

73

enhances the powers of the soul, making it more fitted to serve God. The devil, I believe, wants us to think we are humble and so have no trust in God's goodness. When tempted in this way, cease to think about your unworthiness – think instead of the mercy and love of God and all that he has suffered for us.

W.P. XXXIX

Deceived by the devil?

Someone who previously had helped me and from time to time heard my confession, began saying I was obviously deceived by the devil. And so I was told to make the sign of the cross whenever I saw a vision and to snap my fingers at it in contempt, so as to convince myself that it came from the devil, after which it would not return. I was not to be afraid : God would protect me.

Nevertheless this distressed me greatly, for I could not cease to believe that the visions came from God, and to treat them in such a way would be a shocking thing to do. Besides, I did not want to be deprived of the visions.

L. XXIX

To have to snap my fingers at a vision in which I saw the Lord grieved me deeply. I simply could not accept that the vision came from the devil – not though I were to be chopped into pieces. This was indeed a penance and a heavy one. And so – not to have to make the sign of the cross continually, I used to carry a cross in my hand. This I did nearly all the time. As to snapping my fingers, I was less scrupulous about that.

L. XXIV

5. SOME TIRESOME AND PECULIAR
PERSONS

We are none of us so perfect that we do not feel an antipathy to some people and a great liking for others.

> To P. Jerónimo Gracián, Seville;
> from Toledo, September 1576

I have been talking to Padre Gracián about the postulant the Archbishop wants to send you. I'm really annoyed you should be pestered in this way. The Archbishop shows so little understanding. Padre Gracián says she is a *beata* who suffers spells of acute depression. Experience should have warned us against taking persons of that kind.

> To M. María de San José, Seville;
> from Toledo, July 1577

Isabel de San Jerónimo will have to be made to eat meat for a few days and give up prayer. She has an unstable imagination which makes her believe she actually sees and hears the things she meditates on.

> To P. Jerónimo Gracián, Seville;
> from Toledo, October 1576

I have known persons who, after living for years an

upright and orderly life, have, in the face of difficulties become so restless and depressed that they have utterly exasperated me. Indeed, I have felt quite afraid of them. It is useless to give them advice. They have lived virtuously for so long that they feel entitled to teach others.

I cannot find – and have never been able to – a way to console them, apart from saying I'm extremely sorry, as indeed I am. It is useless to argue. They brood over their troubles and are convinced they are suffering for God's sake. It does not occurr to them that their troubles are of their own making.

I.C. III ii

There are nuns who think themselves so unbelievably perfect that everything they set eyes on appears wrong: it is always these who have the greatest faults.

V.C.

You will appreciate how tedious are these regulations untroduced by Padre Fray Juan de Jesús who, as far as I can see, is going over the same ground that was covered by your constitutions. I cannot imagine why. My nuns are afraid we shall get troublesome superiors who will impose unduly heavy burdens. That will get us nowhere. It is a strange state of affairs if visitors think they have not done their duty unless they bring in new regulations.

Even to read the regulations exhausted me! What, then, would it be like to have to keep them? Believe me, our Rule must not be subject to additions made by tiresome persons; it is all we can do to keep it as it is.

To P. Jerónimo Gracián;
from Toledo, November 1576

I was in a house of ours where the prioress was obsessed with penance, and consequently imposed penances on all the nuns. She used to discipline the entire community by making them recite together the seven penitential psalms as well as other prayers and devotions. That is what happens if a prioress is too taken up with prayer: she keeps the whole community reciting prayers outside prescribed hours – even after matins, when they ought to be in bed asleep.

F. XVIII

This woman and two others I have known (they have just come to mind) were saints in their own estimation. But when I got to know them better they frightened me more than all the sinners I have ever encountered!

C.L.G. II

It would be a thousand times better not to make foundations at all than to take nuns who suffer from melancholia and so play havoc with the entire community.

To P. Jerónimo Gracián;
from Malaga, December 1579

I was amused at what your Reverence said about your being able to sum up that woman as soon as you saw her! You cannot sum up women as easily as that! We make our confessions year in and year out and even so our confessors are astonished to find out how little they have learnt about us.

To P. Ambrosio Mariano de San Benito;
from Toledo, 21 October 1576

Don Pedro has already brought up to me the possibility you mention of his living in one of our priories. It is quite out of the question. They do not take laymen. Besides, he would not put up with the food. As it is he sends away the meat he is given at the inn – unless it is well cooked and highly seasoned : he makes do with a slice of pie. Whenever I can, I send him some little thing, but it is not very often. I don't know anyone who would put up with him and provide just what he fancies.

His disposition is a dreadful affliction – for himself and all concerned. May God bless you, I pray, and preserve you from having to take him back to your home !

To Don Lorenzo de Cepeda, Ávila;
from Toledo April 1580

It's a great mistake to suppose you know everything, and then say you are humble !

To M. María Bautista, Valladolid;
from Seville, August 1575

I simply don't understand some sorts of sanctity. I'm thinking of the person who won't write to you. The other one annoys me, too, who says everything must be done in the way he thinks best.

To P. Jerónimo Gracián;
from Ávila, December 1581

My Lord Bishop, when you have so many saints to deal with, you are beginning to waken to the fact that some of us are far from being saints. And that's why you are forgetting all about me. None the less you may discover in heaven that you are less indebted to those saints than you are to this sinner!

> To Don Álvaro de Mendoza, Bishop of Ávila;
> from Alba de Tormes, February 1574

Jacob did not cease to be a saint because he had to tend his flocks, nor did Abraham nor Joachim.'

> To Don Lorenzo de Cepeda, Ávila;
> from Toledo, January 1577

Charming, I must say, that you should be so constantly in the confessional – and this after your being so unwell. As though you had not enough to do as it is. It's too much for anyone. After all we mustn't expect God to work miracles! Remember that you are not made of iron. Many of the best brains in the community have been destroyed through overwork.

> To P. Jerónimo Gracián, Seville;
> from Toledo, January 1577

Before I forget, I was glad to have the memorandum you sent about the alms you received and your calculations as to what you have earned. I only hope you are speaking the truth. I would be overjoyed to think you were, but you're such a fox! I suspect some subterfuge!

> To M. María de San José, Seville;
> from Toledo, January 1577

God save me from the kind of people who would rather have their own way than do as they are asked!

To Doña Juana de Ahumada;
from Ávila, September 1572

An eccentric saint

The Lord thought fit to awaken in Peter of Alcantara an affection for me, so that this man of God might stand up on my behalf and encourage me at a time of great need.

For forty years, I think he told me, he had slept no more than an hour and a half a night: the overcoming of sleep had been, he said, the hardest part of his penitential life. Such sleep as he had he took sitting down, his head resting on a piece of wood fastened into the wall. He could not have slept lying down even if he had wanted to, for his cell, as is well known, was only four and a half feet long.

During all these years, no matter how hot the sun, how heavy the rain, he did not wear a hood. He wore a garment made of sack cloth and over it a cloak of the same material. When it was very cold, he would take off the cloak, he told me, and leave open the window and the door of his cell, so that when he put the cloak on again, he would get some satisfaction from the increase of warmth. It was quite usual for him to eat only once in three days. When I showed surprise at this he said that, when one became used to it, it was quite possible. Moreover one of his brethren told me that sometimes he went for a whole week without food.

He said that he once spent three years in a house of

his order, yet could not recognise a single friar except from the tone of voice, for he never lifted his eyes and could only go from one part of the house to another by following in the footsteps of his brethren.

He was very old when I got to know him; he looked as if he were made out of the roots of trees. But despite all his piety he was most affable. . . .

When he knew that his life was drawing to a close, he repeated the psalm: '*Laetatus sum in his quae dicta sunt*', knelt down, and died.

V. XXVII

6. CONTEMPLATION, MYSTICAL PHENOMENA AND THE LIKE

Martha and Mary

Martha was holy, but we hear nothing about her being a contemplative. What better could you want than to be like that woman who was thought worthy to receive Christ in her home, prepare meals for him, serve him, even eat at the table with him? If she had been absorbed in contemplation, as was Mary Magdalen, who would have prepared the meal for the heavenly guest? . . .

Remember there must be someone to cook the meals and be happy if you are able to serve as was Martha. Bear in mind that true humility largely consists in being ready for whatever the Lord wants to do with you – be happy whatever he should want and know that you are unworthy to be called his servants. If contemplation, mental prayer, vocal prayer, caring for the sick, serving in the house and working at the lowliest tasks are all ways of attending the Guest who comes to stay with us, eats with us and relaxes with us, then what matter whether we do one task or another?

W.P. XVII

God walks among the pots and pans.

F. V

It is not for us to say what we shall do, but whatever the task, to carry it out as best we can. The choice rests not with us but with the Lord. Be sure to do what is in your power, and if he does not grant you contemplation know that he has laid up this joy for you in heaven. And remember, as I have said before, that he is treating you as if you were strong – giving you, as he gave to himself a cross to bear.

What surer pledge of friendship could there be than to give to you what he gave to himself? His decisions are his own : it is not for us to meddle. Indeed it is well the choice is not ours. If it were, we would all choose to be contemplatives, supposing this to be a more restful way of life !

W.P. XVII

Progress in the spiritual life has nothing to do with consolations granted during prayer – nothing to do with raptures, visions and the like, the value of which we cannot estimate until we reach the world to come. The other things of which I have spoken are, so to speak, 'current coin'; an unfailing source of revenue, a lasting heritage – not payments liable to cease at any moment, as are those which, suddenly bestowed are no less suddenly snatched away.

W.P. XVIII

A castle made from a diamond

I began to think of the soul as a castle made from a single diamond, shining like crystal, in which there are many dwelling places, just as in heaven there are many mansions.

Now let us picture this castle with its many mansions, some above, others below, others at either side – and in the centre, in the midst of them all the most important mansion where secret things pass between God and the soul.

You should not think of those mansions as being just in a row, one behind the other. Rather fix your attention on the central one, the room that belongs to the King. Think of a *palmito*. The succulent part deep within is enclosed by outer rinds which have to be stripped away before the centre can be eaten. When we speak of the soul we should imagine it as spacious, roomy, lofty. And this is no exaggeration, for the soul's capacity is greater than we realise. Moreover this Sun which is in the centre lights up with its radiance every corner of the castle.

It is important to understand this – for the soul which engages in prayer, whether little or much, should not be constrained or cramped. Since God has so honoured it, it should be left free to roam through these mansions, those above and below and on either side. It should not be compelled to stay for a long time in any one room – unless it be to acquire self-knowledge, for at no stage can we dispense with self-knowledge.

I.C. I ii

Be sensible about mystical phenomena

Though some such phenomena may be genuine, I'm sure it is best to regard them of no importance. You and Padre Gracián should do the same. Treat them, then, as being of no account whatsoever for even supposing they are genuine, nothing will be lost. You should, I think, take the line that God guides some people in one way, some in another, and that this particular path is not the one which leads to the greatest sanctity – for this is the truth.

To M. María de San José, Seville;
from Ávila, June 1578

Superiors should not, in general, allow nuns who are neurotic to spend long stretches of time at prayer. Usually the imagination of such persons is their weak point and too much prayer only does harm. Besides, they get extraordinary ideas which neither they themselves nor others who hear of such goings on can possibly understand.

F. VII

Once when I was reciting the Hours with the community I suddenly became recollected and my soul, it seemed to me, was bright all over, like a mirror, completely untarnished, and in its centre a picture of Christ our Lord as I usually imagine him.

This kind of vision, which can come when we are in a state of recollection, is beneficial, for it teaches that the Lord dwells in the innermost part of the soul. Such a meditation is more beneficial, more lasting in its effect, than if we think of God as outside ourselves, as do certain authors of books about prayer. St Augustine makes this point well when he explains how he found God not in the market place nor in any pleasurable pursuits nor in any region in which he sought him, but within himself.

L. XL

One day when I was holding in my hand the cross of a rosary the Lord put out his hand and took it from me. When he gave it back there were four large stones more precious than diamonds – infinitely more so, for it is utterly impossible to compare the natural with the supernatural : diamonds are no better than a counterfeit when set beside the precious stones I saw in that vision. And on the cross in exquisite workmanship were represented the five wounds. I would always see them like that, the Lord told me.

L. XXIV

After Compline, when we were praying in choir, I saw the Blessed Virgin in radiant glory, wearing a white cloak beneath which it seemed she was sheltering us all.

L. XXXVI

One night there came upon me a spiritual impulse of such vehemence that I had no strength to resist it. I thought I was being carried up to heaven. There, the first persons I saw were my father and mother. And such amazing things happened in so short a time – no longer than it would take to say a *Hail Mary* – that I was swept utterly out of myself and felt this favour was indeed too great to be endured.

I was afraid it might be an illusion. And yet it did not seem so at all. I did not know what to do. I was ashamed to go to my confessor – not out of any humility but for fear he would laugh at me and say : 'Quite a St Paul with her heavenly visions ! Quite a St Jerome !' However, in the end I went to him. For although it was hard to talk about these things I did not dare keep silent, so afraid was I that I was being deceived.

When my confessor saw how upset I was he did much to reassure me, and gave me several good reasons for my having no need to worry.

L. XXXVIII

God can reveal himself when it is his will to do so. He does not need our puny efforts. Despite ourselves, he transports the soul as easily as might a giant take up a piece of straw : it is useless to resist him. It would indeed be odd were we to suppose that if God willed a toad to fly, he would wait for the creature to do so of its own efforts !

L. XXII

Once, while I was praying, the Lord deigned to reveal to me his hands. Their beauty was beyond all words. A few days later I saw his face. This left me completely wrapt in thought. I wondered why he revealed himself gradually (later I saw his entire person), until I realised that he was taking compassion on my human weakness. He knew (may he be blessed for ever !) that so much glory revealed at once would have been more than a creature as unworthy as I could have borne. And so, in his mercy, he prepared me little by little.

L. XXVIII

God does not allow us to drink of the water of perfect contemplation just when we like. The choice does not rest with us. This divine union is something supernatural, granted to cleanse the soul, to leave it untainted.

W.P. XIX

A rapture, as a rule, comes upon one with so sudden and strong an impulse that it is not possible to be fore-warned or to put up a resistance. You see and feel this cloud – or rather a mighty powerful eagle that soars aloft bearing you on its wings.

L. XX

I've had raptures again. They're most embarrassing. Several times in public – during Matins, for instance. I'm so ashamed. I simply want to hide away somewhere !

To Don Lorenzo de Cepeda;
from Toledo, January 1577

The Trinity

The revelation I received comprises three separate Persons, each of whom can be seen by himself, each of whom speaks. The Son, I have been reflecting, alone took human flesh that this truth might be made manifest. These Persons have mutual love, communication and knowledge, each in relation to the others. If, then, each in himself is one Person how can we say and believe that all three are one essence – a truth I would die a thousand times to defend? In the three Persons there is one will, one power, one sovereignty, so that no one of them can do anything apart from the other two. Therefore however many creatures there may be, there is one Creator only.

Could the Son create an ant without the Father? No, for the power of the three is one.

S.R. XXXIII

The Prayer of Quiet

The Prayer of Quiet is a supernatural state.

Whatever our efforts we cannot reach it of ourselves, for it is a state in which the soul enters into peace or rather in which the Lord by his presence bestows peace upon us, as he bestowed it upon the holy Simeon. All the faculties of the soul are still. Moreover, in a manner in no way related to the senses, the soul knows that it is close to God – that if it were a little closer it would be one with him through union. This does not mean that the soul sees God with either bodily or spiritual eyes.

Simeon did not see the Son of God. He saw a child in swaddling clothes who could have been the son of the simple pair who brought him. It was the child who revealed himself to Simeon. In a like manner, though with less clarity, the soul realises that it is in the Kingdom – or close to the King who will bestow upon it the Kingdom – and such awe comes upon it that it dares not ask for anything. It is, so to speak, bemused both inwardly and outwardly. The body (that is the outer man) has no wish to move : it rests in the manner of one who has reached his journey's end so that, its strength redoubled, it may once more set forth on its way.

It is not the body alone that experiences a sense of delight. The soul, too, feels a deep satisfaction. It is so thankful to find itself near the fountain that, even before it has drunk of this water, it has already had its fill.

W.P. XXXI

In this mansion all is different. Our God in his goodness thinks fit to remove the scales from the eyes of the soul that it may see and understand, though in a small way, the favour which is bestowed on it. This happens in a manner that for us is strange. For the soul is brought into this mansion by means of an intellectual vision in which, the truth being presented in a special way, the Holy Trinity reveals itself in its three Persons. First the soul is enkindled – illumined, so to say – by a cloud of great brightness. It sees the three Persons separately, and yet, by the unusual knowledge granted to it, realises that, without any doubt whatsoever, all three Persons are one substance, one power, one knowledge, one God. Thus what we believe by faith the soul comprehends, we may say, by sight, although nothing is in fact perceived by the eyes of the body or the soul. All three Persons reveal themselves to the soul, speak to the soul, and make clear the words attributed in the Gospel to the Lord – namely, that he and the Father and the Holy Spirit will come to dwell within the soul which loves him and keeps his commandments.

I.C. VII i

The Holy Spirit is, I believe, the intermediary between the soul and God, moving the soul with such ardour that it becomes enkindled with the supreme fire.

C.L.G. V

Union

In the union that is sometimes called spiritual marriage the Lord reveals himself in the centre of the soul by means not of an imaginary but an intellectual vision (something more subtle than anything of which we have yet spoken) just as he appeared to the Apostles without entering through a door when he said to them 'Peace be to you'.

I.C. VII ii

When we speak of union we might think of a pair of wax candles joined together in such a manner that the light they give is one: the wicks of the candles, the wax, and the light are one. And yet afterwards each candle can without difficulty be separated from the other and the candles become two again.

ibid.

Or let us think of water. Rain is falling into a river or a spring. There is nothing except water nor is it possible to separate the water in the river from that which falls from the sky. Or imagine a tiny stream which flows into the sea from which it can no longer be separate.

ibid.

Or, again, imagine a room that has two large windows through which the light streams. The light enters by different windows, yet it is one and the same light.

ibid.

Moses could not describe all he saw in the bush, but only as much as God willed. If God had not revealed these secrets in a manner which enabled him to realise their truth – so that he might know and believe in God's presence – Moses would not have taken upon himself those many arduous tasks. Amid the thorns of the bush he learned many wonderful things which gave him the courage to work on behalf of the people of Israel. Therefore we must not search for reasons to enable us to understand the hidden ways of God. Rather, believing, as indeed we do, in his supreme power, we must realise that it is not possible for us, unworthy as we are, to apprehend his greatness. Let us give thanks that we may understand some part of it!

Let me make a comparison, inadequate though it is. Imagine you have entered the private apartment – what, I think, they call the *camarín* in the palace of a king or one of the nobility – where you see an extraordinary variety of glass and porcelain and all sorts of things displayed in such a manner that, as you enter, you see almost everything at a glance. I was once taken into such a room in the castle of the Duchess of Alba, where I was obliged to stay under obedience.

I was amazed and began to wonder for what purpose all these things were used. Then I realised that the sight of so many things might enable one to give glory to God. I thought how useful this experience could be for my present purpose. For though I was there for sometime, I could not recall everything in detail – only my overall impression.

Even so when God has revealed great things to the soul, it will not be able to describe these nor to apprehend more of the supernatural than he is pleased to permit.

I.C. VI. iv

Holy Communion

At times I have felt a longing to receive Holy Communion so vehemently that I doubt if I can put this into words.

One morning the rain was deluging down so heavily that I did not know if I could leave the house. Yet, once I had set out, so overwhelming was my longing that if the raindrops had been spears levelled at my breast I would, I believe, have thrust my way through. How little, then, did drops of water matter!

When I reached the church I went into a deep rapture. I saw – so it appeared – not a gate into heaven, as I have at other times, but Heaven wide open. There was revealed to me the throne I had seen previously and, above it, another (I did not see this with my eyes but in a manner that defies description) on which was God himself. The throne, it seemed to me, was upheld by beasts: I have heard something, I think, about these creatures – they might have been, I reflected, the Evangelists.

I could not see what the throne was like or who was seated upon it. I saw only a multitude of angels incomparably more beautiful, I thought than those I had seen in heaven. I wondered if they were seraphim or cherubim for their glory was beyond anything I had ever known: they were, it appeared, ablaze with fire. There is a considerable difference between angels, as I had discovered before, and the glory I felt within me on this occasion was such that it cannot find expression in the written word, or in converse, or be imagined by anyone who has not experienced it. It was as though all that can be desired were there at one and the same time. And yet I saw nothing with my own eyes. I was told – I do not know by whom – that the most I could do was to understand my inability to understand and realise that all else compared with this is as nothing.

L. XXXIX

7. CONVENTS OF THE REFORM

St Joseph's, Ávila

It is quite wrong, believe me, that large houses should be built from the money of the poor. God forbid! Our convents should be small and poor in every sense. We must try in some degree to resemble our King. What had he? The stable in Bethlehem in which he was born, and the cross on which he died – little comfort had these to offer.

W.P. II

As for an elaborate convent with grandiose buildings – God preserve us! Don't forget that on the day of judgment all will come crashing down – and who can say how soon that will be? It would hardly look well if a convent containing just thirteen women were to contribute to such a din!

ibid.

The convent, the Lord told me, would be founded and in it great service done to him. It would be called St Joseph's: St Joseph would keep watch at one door, Our Lady at the other. Christ would be with us and our convent give forth its radiance like a star.

L. XXXII

Medina del Campo

When the news of this foundation got around in Ávila there was a lot of spiteful gossip. Some people said I was out of my mind, others that such folly would surely come to an untimely end. The Bishop (he told me this himself later) thought it the height of folly, but did not say so because he was very fond of me and did not want to cause me distress.

F. III

We reached Medina del Campo at midnight on the vigil of the feast of Our Lady in August. Not to disturb anyone we got out at the monastery of St Ana and went the rest of the way on foot. Thanks be to God we met no one – for they were just shutting in the bulls in readiness for the bull-fight on the next day.

Having come to the house we went into the courtyard. The walls, I noticed, were in a tumbledown condition. The Lord must have thought fit that the Father who found us this house should be blind or else he would have realised that it was not a suitable place to put the Blessed Sacrament. When I looked at the porch I saw we would have to remove some of the earth in it. Also there were holes in the roof and the walls were not plastered. The night was nearly over and we had little in the way of hangings – three in all, I think it was. But by the mercy of God the steward of the lady who was the owner had quite a lot of tapestry and a blue damask bedspread which she said was to be given to us.

We did not know what to do about nails. It was too

early to buy any. So we looked around the walls and after some trouble, found enough. Then the hangings were put up while we, the nuns, proceeded to clean the floor. We worked so hard that by daybreak the altar was ready.

F. III

I always left men to guard the Blessed Sacrament. But for fear they might fall asleep, I used to get up in the night and look at the Sacrament out of the window.

When the moon shone I could see it easily.

ibid.

Toledo

For some days we had no beds apart from the mattresses and one blanket, and not so much as a scrap of brush-wood on which to cook a sardine.

F. XV

Salamanca

The students had left the house in such a mess that we had to work all night. Early in the morning the first Mass was said.

F. XIX

On the night of All Souls I was alone except for one companion. I have to laugh when I think of the fears of this nun. Because the house was spacious and roomy and had a lot of attics, she could not get the students out of her head. As they had been annoyed at having to move out,

97

she thought that one of them might perhaps be in hiding. So we shut ourselves into a room where there was straw – this was the first thing I used to get when founding a convent, for then we were not without a bed. And so we slept on the straw, with two or three blankets that had been lent to us.

ibid

When my companion realised that she was shut into the room, her fears abated somewhat. Nevertheless she kept peering first in one direction, then in another. 'Why do you keep looking around?' I asked. 'No one could possibly get in.' 'Mother', she replied, 'I'm wondering what you would do all alone here, if I were to die.' It was, I admit, an alarming thought. I became quite frightened. The bells were tolling, for, as I have said it was the vigil of All Souls. And the devil if he can't frighten us in one way, finds another. 'Well,' I said to the sister, 'I'll think about that problem when it arises. Meanwhile let me go to sleep!'

ibid.

On the way to Seville

I must say something about the terrible inn. They gave us a cubby-hole roofed like a shed. There was no window and every time the door opened the sun poured in. The heat in Andalusia is quite different from our Castilian heat – much more trying. Because I was ill, they made me lie down on a bed, but it was so full of bumps that I would rather have lain on the ground. I don't know how I endured it – it was as if the bed were filled with sharp stones! What a nuisance bad health can be! It is easy enough to put up with things when one is well.

In the end I thought it better to get up and continue on our way. At least the sun in the open air would be preferable to this cubby-hole.

F. XXIV

I would have died of fright ...

I must tell you the dreadful thing that happened to me. We were sitting by a heap of corn near an inn where there was no room for us and having quite a nice time. Then, suddenly, a great salamander or lizard of some kind came out of the corn and darted up my arm between the sleeve of my tunic and the flesh. By God's mercy it got no further or I think I would have died of fright. My brother snatched hold of it and flung it away. Even so, it caught Antonio Ruiz on the mouth.

To P. Jerónimo Gracián;
from Malaga, June 1576

Cordoba (on the way to Seville)

We travelled at a good pace so as to reach Cordoba early in the morning and hear Mass without drawing attention to ourselves. There was a church the far side of the bridge, we were told, if we wanted to be alone.

However, just as we were about to cross we found that a licence was needed for carriages and could be obtained only from the Governor. It took us more than two hours to get this, for no one was up! Crowds gathered to find out who we were. And when, at last, the licence was granted, the carriages could not get through the gate at the end of the bridge. A way had to be sawn through – or something of the kind. It took ages!

At long last we came to the church where Julián de Ávila was to say Mass. It was Pentecost and the church which was dedicated to the Holy Spirit (we had not known this) was absolutely packed.

I was extremely worried and thought, in the circumstances, it would be more sensible to go on our way without hearing Mass, rather than be caught up in this tumult. Julián de Ávila, however, did not agree and as he was a theologian we felt we must defer. When we got out of the carriages near the church no one could see our faces because we wore large veils. Still, the sight of us in our white frieze cloaks and hemp-soled shoes caused no end of a commotion – such a commotion that you would have imagined the church was being invaded by a herd of bulls!

F. XXIV

No one would have believed that in a city as wealthy as Seville we received less help in making our foundation than in any other place. Sometimes I thought I would have to abandon the entire project. Perhaps it is something to do with the climate of these parts, but here, I have always heard it said, God allows the devils more power to tempt us. They certainly harrassed me. I've never found myself more cowardly in all my life!

F. XXV

There is not a more attractive house or positon in the whole of Seville. I don't think we shall feel the heat. The